Growth Through Virtue

Month by Month with Saint Alphonsus Liguori

Daniel L. Lowery, C.SS.R.

One Liguori Drive
Liguori, Missouri 63057
(314) 464-2500

Imprimi Potest:
John F. Dowd, C.SS.R.
Provincial, St. Louis Province
Redemptorist Fathers

Imprimatur:
+ Edward J. O'Donnell
Vicar General, Archdiocese of St. Louis

ISBN 0-89243-222-5

Copyright © 1984, Liguori Publications
Printed in U.S.A.

All rights reserved. No part of this book may be reproduced, stored in a retrieval system, or transmitted without the written permission of Liguori Publications.

Scripture texts in this work are taken from the NEW AMERICAN BIBLE, copyright © 1970, by the Confraternity of Christian Doctrine, Washington, D.C., and are used by permission of copyright owner. All rights reserved.

Excerpts from VATICAN II: THE CONCILIAR AND POSTCONCILIAR DOCUMENTS, edited by Austin Flannery, O.P., copyright © 1975, Costello Publishing Company, Northport, NY, are used by permission of publisher. All rights reserved.

Excerpts from FOUNDATIONS OF CHRISTIAN FAITH by Karl Rahner. English translation copyright © 1978 by The Crossroad Publishing Company. Reprinted by permission.

Contents

Foreword 5

JANUARY: Faith, the First Gift 8

FEBRUARY: Hope, the Hidden Gift 12

MARCH: Love of God, the Greatest Gift 17

APRIL: Love of Neighbor, the Unselfish Gift 21

MAY: Poverty, the Enriching Gift 26

JUNE: Chastity, the Personal Gift 30

JULY: Obedience, the Liberating Gift 35

AUGUST: Humility, the Honest Gift 40

SEPTEMBER: Mortification, the Renewing Gift 45

OCTOBER: Recollection, the Enlightening Gift 50

NOVEMBER: Prayer, the Unifying Gift 54

DECEMBER: Love of the Cross, the Redemptive Gift 59

Foreword

Saint Alphonsus Liguori (1696-1787) was a man of many and varied accomplishments.

From his earliest years he was a brilliant scholar. In the course of his life he wrote a large number of books and articles on theology and the spiritual life. Because his books were, and are, so sound in doctrine and so popular with so many different groups of people, he was declared a Doctor of the Church in 1871. This revered title has been conferred on only a limited number of theologians in the long history of the Church.

In his mature years Saint Alphonsus dedicated himself especially to the study of moral theology. He wrote a classical four-volume work in moral theology for the guidance of priests and confessors. He was, and is, widely admired for the way he kept a middle position between rigorism on the one hand and laxism on the other. For his outstanding contributions in the field of moral theology, the Church named him the Patron of Moralists and Confessors.

In 1732 Alphonsus Liguori founded the Congregation of the Most Holy Redeemer, also known as the Redemptorists. This worldwide community of religious men shares in the charism of Saint Alphonsus and tries to carry on his work of "bringing the Good News to the poor." (Liguori Publications, named in honor of the saint, aims at continuing what he called "the apostolate of the pen.")

It is safe to say that the major pastoral concern of Saint Alphonsus was the spiritual growth of ordinary people. His great joy was to preach the Gospel and to explain Catholic teaching in language and images people could readily understand. His preaching and writing were characterized by a personal, practical, down-to-earth approach. In the deepest sense of the word, Saint Alphonsus was "a pastor of souls."

One of the key emphases in the spiritual direction of Saint Alphonsus may be labeled "growth through virtue." The Christian is called to imitate the life and virtues of Jesus Christ, to "put on" Christ in his or her way of thinking and acting. In accord with the Catholic tradition, Saint Alphonsus saw the three theological (God-directed) virtues of faith, hope, and charity as pure gifts of grace: gifts of God given to us with sanctifying grace so that we can live and act on the supernatural level. At the same time, he saw the moral virtues, many and varied as they are, as gifts that enable us to shape our conscious behavior according to the law of God as revealed to us by Jesus.

In characteristic fashion, Saint Alphonsus proposed a practical plan that could help the ordinary person grow in this imitation of Christ. He recommended the practice of "the virtue of the month": that is, highlighting one of the key Christian virtues in a given month and giving special attention to that virtue in one's reading, reflection, prayer, and daily living.

This booklet presents "the virtue of the month" according to the pattern proposed by Saint Alphonsus. I want to make it clear, however, that this booklet in no way pretends to offer the complete theology of Saint Alphonsus on any single virtue. There is no substitute for reading his original works. In each of the virtues I have simply tried to highlight what I believe to be his most characteristic and significant viewpoints. I have tried to be faithful to the practical approach of the saint and have quoted liberally from his writings.

Since it is not possible in this small booklet to unveil the total theology of Saint Alphonsus on the meaning of grace and redemption, I thought it wise to treat some of the virtues — for example, faith and hope — in the context of Vatican II. In presenting other virtues — for example, poverty and obedience — I realized that the treatment of Saint Alphonsus was especially directed to men and women of religious communities. In these cases, I took the liberty of including reflections that would also apply to the laity of the Church. In all cases, however, I sincerely hope that I have caught "the spirit of Saint Alphonsus" in what I have written.

At the end of each chapter in this booklet I have included some "practical suggestions" that may be of help to the reader. There is a suggested practice for each week of the month. It goes without saying that many other suggestions could be offered. I am sure that creative users of this booklet will come up with many different ways of applying "the virtue of the month" to the concrete circumstances of their lives. The important point, frequently stressed by Saint Alphonsus, is that the virtues are not theoretical constructs to be admired but gifts to be used in living the Christian life.

The material in this booklet appeared, in slightly different form, in the *Liguorian*. I thank the editor, Norman Muckerman, C.SS.R., for permission to reprint it in this form. I owe a special word of thanks to Christopher Farrell, C.SS.R., for preparing this booklet for publication.

As a son of Saint Alphonsus, I am happy to offer these reflections to a wider audience. I hope that all who use them will experience spiritual growth through "the virtue of the month" and so come closer to the imitation of Jesus Christ who is our way, our truth, and our life.

— Daniel L. Lowery, C.SS.R.

January

Faith, the First Gift

Last Sunday at the Mass I celebrated we sang the lively hymn:
Faith of our fathers, holy faith
We will be true to thee till death!

Later in the afternoon, watching a football game, I heard the announcer say: "It's hard for the cornerbacks to cover those fast receivers. I hope the cornerbacks *don't lose faith* in themselves."

That evening, while I was sharing a pizza with several priest friends, the conversation drifted to preaching. One of the priests remarked: "In my opinion, a good sermon should help people see that their *faith* is not separated from their real life."

From these simple examples — and they could be multiplied — it is clear that the term *faith* has a number of different meanings. But don't go away. In this brief chapter I won't try to explain all of them! In considering faith as our monthly virtue for January, however, I want to dwell on one helpful distinction frequently made in Catholic theology. I refer to the distinction between faith as "a body of truth revealed by God" (Christian doctrine) and faith as "a personal response to that revelation" (the virtue of faith).

God's Revelation

First of all, faith is possible only because God has graciously revealed himself and his truth to us. By our own unaided reason we could never come to the full knowledge of God and his truth. Though God has revealed himself in many ways, the fullness of his revelation is in Jesus Christ. "In times past, God spoke in fragmentary and varied ways to our fathers through the prophets; in this, the final age, he has spoken to us through his Son, whom he has made heir of all things and through whom he first created the universe. This Son is the reflection of the Father's glory, the exact representation of the Father's being, and he sustains all things by his powerful word" (Hebrews 1:1-3).

Everything about Jesus reveals God to us, for he "completed and perfected Revelation and confirmed it with divine guarantees. He did this by the total fact of his presence and self-manifestation — by words and works, signs and miracles, but above all by his death and glorious resurrection from the dead, and finally by sending the spirit of truth" (Vatican II, *Divine Revelation*, 4).

The Church of Christ

Like a priceless treasure, this full revelation of God was entrusted to the loving care of the Church. "The one mediator, Christ, established and ever sustains here on earth his holy Church, the community of faith, hope and charity, as a visible organization through which he communicates truth and grace to all men" (Vatican II, *The Church*, 8). The Church's authority in matters of faith is not arbitrary, but "is exercised in the name of Jesus Christ." Moreover, the Church's teaching authority "is not superior to the Word of God, but is its servant. It teaches only what has been handed on to it" (Vatican II, *Divine Revelation*, 10).

The revelation of God, true Christian doctrine, the content of faith — these are found in their fullness in the Church, guided and protected, for the sake of God's pilgrim people, by the Holy Spirit.

Our Response to God's Revelation

The virtue of faith is our human response to this revelation of God. It is one of the three theological (God-directed) virtues: "There are in the end three things that last: faith, hope, and love, and the greatest of these is love" (1 Corinthians 13:13).

How are we to understand this virtue of faith?

In a panoramic description, Vatican II explains: "By faith man freely commits his entire self to God, making 'the full submission of his intellect and will to God who reveals,' and willingly assenting to the Revelation given by him. Before this faith can be exercised, man must have the grace of God to move and assist him; he must have the interior helps of the Holy Spirit, who moves the heart and converts it to God, who opens the eyes of the mind and 'makes it easy for all to accept and believe the truth.' The same Holy Spirit constantly perfects faith by his gifts, so that Revelation may be more and more profoundly understood" (*Divine Revelation*, 5).

Christian Affirmations

This tightly packed description, when patiently unpacked, yields a number of Christian affirmations about faith:

— Faith is a gift of God; it is possible only through God's helping grace.

— Faith is a free human act; God does not force the human person to make the act of faith; neither should others.

— Faith is an act of the intellect, an assent to God's truth, "saying yes" to his revelation.

— Faith is not only an act of the intellect but also an act of the will, an act informed by love, involving a radical self-commitment to God.

— Faith involves obedience to God ("believe and obey" is a regular refrain in Saint Paul's letters), and demands genuine conversion when we have failed in obedience to him.

Practical Suggestions

As we focus on the virtue of faith during January, the following practical suggestions, largely drawn from the writings of Saint Alphonsus, are worthy of attention:

First Week: Read and pray over the story of Abraham, "our father in faith." His magnificent story is told in chapters 12 through 22 of the Book of Genesis.

Second Week: Set aside some time for enlarging or enriching our knowledge of God's revelation. "God wishes us to use our natural powers of intellect to know and be convinced of all that the Holy Church proposes to our belief" (Saint Alphonsus). This might include a planned reading of the Scriptures, a study of the Creed, or a fuller understanding of Catholic teaching as found, for example, in the documents of Vatican II or in a catechism for adults. (See the suggested bibliography at the end of this booklet.)

Third Week: Open ourselves in prayer to the Holy Spirit so that the virtue of faith may grow in us. Prayer is the language of faith. "Let us thank God from the bottom of our hearts for the inestimable gift of faith and never cease asking with the apostles, 'Lord, increase our faith' " (Saint Alphonsus).

Fourth Week: Examine our lives to see in what ways we are not living by faith. If our faith is separated from our life, there's something wrong! "To be pleasing and acceptable in the sight of God it is not enough only to believe all that our holy faith teaches us; we must also regulate our life in accordance with our faith" (Saint Alphonsus). How are we lacking in our obedience to God's will and God's law? What are we going to do about it?

February

Hope, the Hidden Gift

Of all the Christian virtues, hope seems to be the least noticed and the first forgotten. Almost twenty-five years ago the distinguished psychiatrist Karl Menninger pointed out that in a prominent encyclopedia of the time there were many columns on love, and even more on faith, but there was not even a listing on hope!

Hope remains, nonetheless, one of the great theological virtues — one of the gifts God infuses into the soul with sanctifying grace. Though of fundamental importance at all times, this virtue has special relevance in our nuclear age when much of the American "conventional wisdom," so long taken for granted, seems no longer to apply. Hope in its deepest meaning is a virtue which looks to the future, yet does not forget the past nor neglect the present.

Hope and the Future

Hope is centered on God. It is the virtue by which we confidently expect the fullness of glory, our eternal destiny, the face-to-face vision of God. In the words of Saint Alphonsus: "The first and foremost object of our hope, the object by excellence, is the possession of God in heaven." To hope for less than this is to miss the basic Christian message. "If our hopes in Christ are limited to this life only, we are the most pitiable of men" (1 Corinthians 15:19).

Since Christian hope always involves "conviction about things we do not see" (Hebrews 11:1), it is easy enough for secularists to dismiss it. Karl Rahner, S.J., points out that the Christian is one who "professes that the absolute and infinite future is his own future. It is a future which he cannot win for himself all by himself and by his own power, but rather it is a future which gives itself again and again in free grace. . . . Hence he [the Christian] will always be regarded as utopian by the absolute pessimists, and also by those who believe that they are able to be absolute optimists within their own experience of existence" (*Foundations of Christian Faith*, page 405).

In truth, the virtue of hope does not rest on either a natural optimism or a natural pessimism. A sunny disposition may be an attractive quality, but it is not necessary for hope. The umbrella of hope can embrace those who are naturally sad and dyspeptic as well as those who are upbeat and cheerful! For the early Christians the anchor was the favorite symbol of hope (see Hebrews 6:19) because it was the symbol of strength and stability. The stability of our hope comes, however, not from ourselves, not from our optimistic outlook, but rather from our gracious God and from our risen Savior, Jesus Christ: "If we have died with Christ, we believe that we are also to live with him" (Romans 6:8).

Hope and the Past

Some modern Catholics feel that sin has been too much emphasized in the past preaching and teaching of the Church. While it is always possible that sin can be poorly presented by parents or pastoral ministers, it still remains true, as Saint Augustine said, that sin is the one absolute evil in the universe. Grave sin is a fundamental choice against God who is the special object of our hope. Sin is the choice of eternal death rather than eternal life.

The power of sin in our lives, however, cannot overcome the power of hope. In hope we confidently expect the forgiveness of our past sins because of the gracious mercy of our God, because we have been redeemed by the precious blood of Christ. "Realize that you were delivered from the futile way of life your fathers handed on to you, not by any diminishable sum of silver or gold, but by Christ's blood beyond all price . . ." (1 Peter 1:18,19).

Despair, in the Christian meaning of the word, is a loss of hope in God's mercy, a depressing conviction that God cannot or will not forgive our sins. It is the ultimate tragedy because it puts a dark veil over God's most clear revelation about himself:

> Though your sins be like scarlet,
>   they may become white as snow;
> Though they be crimson red,
>   they may become white as wool (Isaiah 1:18).

To all who have truly repented of their sins, Saint Alphonsus directs this vibrant message of hope: "Why are you tortured with fear and distrust? Renew your courage at the sight of so many saints who at one time lived at enmity with God, but returned to him repentant and sorry, full of hope for the pardon of their sins. The same can happen to you!"

Hope and the Present

Hope is not a Pollyannaish kind of virtue. It does not demand that we close our eyes to the real limitations and sufferings of our own lives or to the tragic and twisted events of the world in which we live. Rather, the virtue of hope calls us to affirm that, no matter what sufferings or difficulties we experience, God is always with us.

> For you are at my side
> With your rod and your staff
>   that give me courage (Psalm 23:4).

Father Rahner beautifully captures the paradox of the Christian life when he says: "Christians too know joy at one moment and tears at another. They experience the grandeur and the vitality of human life, and at another moment they taste death, transitoriness and disappointment. But to be able to open oneself to the reality of life freely . . . without absolutizing either earthly life or death, this can be done only by someone who believes and hopes that the totality of the life which we experience is encompassed by the holy mystery of eternal love" (*Foundations of Christian Faith,* page 405).

With a clear eye the Christian sees the darkness that exists in the world. He or she is ready to do all within his or her power to diminish that pattern of darkness but, at the same time, never quits hoping in him who said:

> I am the light of the world.
> No follower of mine shall ever walk
>   in darkness;
> no, he shall possess the light of life (John 8:12).

Practical Suggestions

That the marvelous virtue of hope may grow in us during this month of February, we might implement the following suggestions:

First Week: Read and reflect upon the journey of the chosen people from Egypt to Mount Sinai, with special attention to God's provident care of them. The story is told in chapters 12 through 18 of the Book of Exodus.

Second Week: Feature the Act of Hope in our daily prayers. This Act of Hope may be informal and in our own words, or may be based on this classical formula: "My God, relying on your infinite goodness and promises, I hope to obtain pardon for my sins, the help of your grace and life everlasting, through the merits of Jesus Christ, my Lord and Savior."

Third Week: Avail ourselves of the Sacrament of Penance. This should not be done in a casual manner nor in a frenzy of neurotic guilt, but with confidence that the loving mercy of Christ and reconciliation with God are signed forth to us in this sacrament.

Fourth Week: Make a list of the things that burden or frighten us: ill health, unemployment, loneliness, war, crime, death. Make a conscious effort to "let go" of these fears and worries; and "let God," whose providence still rules our lives and the world.

March

Love of God, the Greatest Gift

The centerpiece of the spirituality of Saint Alphonsus was "the love of God." Steeped as he was in the Scriptures, he saw the virtue of charity as the very heart of the Christian life. Passionate by nature, he committed himself in his life, preaching, and writing to this love.

Reflecting the teaching of the New Testament, Saint Alphonsus liked to distinguish two aspects of this virtue called "the love of God": first, God's great love for us; and second, our love for God in return.

God's Love for Us

Like the sun that rises unbidden each morning to warm the earth, God's love is freely lavished upon each one of us. His love is poured out upon us not because we have proven ourselves worthy of it but because we are "the apple of his eye." The love of God for us is manifested in visible form in the person of Jesus.

God's love was revealed in our midst in this way:
he sent his only Son to the world
that we might have life through him.

Love, then, consists in this:
not that we have loved God
but that he has loved us
and has sent his Son as an offering for our sins
(1 John 4:9-10).

That is the central message of Saint Alphonsus: *Try to remember how much God has loved you!* A typical line from his pen is this: "If the love of all persons, all angels, all saints were combined, they could not equal the smallest part of the love of God for you."

God's love, like a drama in three acts, was shown especially in the Incarnation, death, and Resurrection of Christ. With his feet firmly planted in the rich soil of southern Italy, Saint Alphonsus had no Anglo-Saxon fear of emphasizing external objects to lead us to deeper mysteries. He urged the learned and the unlearned alike to meditate on "the crib, the cross, and the tabernacle." In this "human" way, he felt, we would begin to catch a glimmer of God's warm and tender love for us.

Our Love for God

This free, priceless gift of God to us deserves — fairly cries out for — a response of love on our part. But how can we respond to God's love? There are, to be sure, countless ways; but one of the main ways, in the view of Saint Alphonsus, is the way highlighted by Jesus himself. Of himself Jesus said:

. . . It is not to do my own will
that I have come down from heaven,
but to do the will of him who sent me (John 6:38).

Of his disciples Jesus said: " 'Who is my mother? Who are my brothers?' Then, extending his hand toward his disciples, he said, 'There are my mother and my brothers. Whoever does the will of my heavenly Father is brother and sister and mother to me' " (Matthew 12:48-50).

Echoing this Gospel principle, Saint Alphonsus developed a basic summary (a kind of syllogism) concerning our response to God:

All holiness consists in the love of God;
but the love of God consists in conformity
   to the will of God;
therefore, all holiness consists in conformity
   to the will of God.

But Saint Alphonsus, a traveling missionary and a people-oriented bishop, knew that this "statement of principle" would not be of much help to most people. So he frequently brought it down to the nitty-gritty of life. He pointed out, of course, that God's will is manifested to us principally through the Scriptures, the living Word of God, and through the Church, guided by the Spirit to teach in matters of faith and morals with the authority of God himself. Further, however, the will of God is manifested to us in the duties and responsibilities of our vocation in life — and, very concretely, in the peculiar circumstances of our lives here and now. "The chief point," he wrote, "lies in our embracing the will of God in all things that befall us, not only when they are favorable, but when they are contrary to our wishes. When things go well, even sinners find no difficulty in being in a state of uniformity to God's will; but the saints are in uniformity also under circumstances which run counter to self-love. It is in this that the perfection of our love of God is shown."

For the person who loves God, in other words, nothing happens by chance. Everything about our lives, even our crosses, represent an invitation to love. A contemporary spiritual writer, Dom Hubert Van Zeller, has expressed this in a striking way: "Before the creation of the world, God has thought out the country, class, surroundings, income, relatives, looks and health best suited to the work he wants us to do. Out of millions of years, he has chosen now." Our response to God's love will be here and now, or it will not be at all!

Love Forever

Though sometimes described as a preacher of hell and damnation — and there is no doubt that he did place emphasis on "fear of the Lord as the beginning of wisdom" — still Saint Alphonsus could just as fairly be described as a preacher of heaven! He frequently wrote about heaven as "the perfection of love." "To long for heaven in order to possess God and love him more perfectly is a true and perfect love of God, for eternal glory is the perfection of this love." In heaven we will finally be able to appreciate without time-bound limits the infinite love of God for us. Saint Alphonsus would surely have agreed with the dying words of Prince Andrey, in *War and Peace*: "All is bound up in love alone. Love is God, and dying means for me a particle of love, to go back to the universal and eternal source of love."

Practical Suggestions

To highlight the love of God this March, these practical suggestions may be of help to us:

First Week: Meditate on the sufferings and death of Jesus as described in chapters 26 and 27 of Saint Matthew's Gospel. Saint Alphonsus saw the crucifix as a moving sign of God's love for us. "How could our Lord have better proved his love for us than by suffering so much pain and such contempt and by ending his life in bitter agony on the cross?"

Second Week: Emphasize gratitude and thanksgiving in our daily prayer. "Because of the love God bears us, he is deserving of our deepest gratitude. We should never cease giving thanks to God who has loved us so much!"

Third Week: Pinpoint one area of our lives where we are struggling against God's will. The usual cause of this is selfishness. In the words of Alphonsus: "Selfishness makes many demands against true love; we must learn to say no to selfishness."

Fourth Week: Discern in a prayerful manner what God may be asking of us as a fuller response to his love. For example, are we being called to a fuller and richer prayer life? Are we being asked to commit our time and talent and treasure more completely to the building up of God's Kingdom?

April

Love of Neighbor, the Unselfish Gift

Some years ago, in the small town where I was stationed, I became friends with a retired Baptist minister. Known to everyone as "The Preacher," he was a man of rich experience and wide-ranging interests. He especially delighted in good conversation — about the Bible, the Church, trends and changes in society. In our conversations he would often pose a question. The answer — whatever it was — would provide a jumping-off point for further questions!

He once asked me to consider this question: "If you took up the New Testament for the first time — without any previous exposure to it — what do you think would strike you most forcefully?" I offered several responses, but not, apparently, the one he was looking for. "No, Daniel," he said, "the thing that would strike you most forcefully would be the teaching of Jesus on neighborly love!"

The more I have thought about that, the more I am convinced that "The Preacher" was right! Like the floats in a giant parade, the sayings of Jesus on love of neighbor just keep rolling off the pages of the Gospels. But as with floats, we can almost take them for granted and look at them with a jaundiced eye. We need a fresh eye and an ear freshly attuned to what he is telling us.

The Law of Love

With incisive clarity Jesus summarizes the great law — the law of love — upon which the entire Hebrew and Christian traditions stand. "On one occasion a lawyer stood up to pose him this problem: 'Teacher, what must I do to inherit everlasting life?' Jesus answered him: 'What is written in the law? How do you read it?' He replied:

'You shall love the Lord your God
with all your heart,
with all your soul,
with all your strength,
and with all your mind;
and your neighbor as yourself.'

Jesus said, 'You have answered correctly. Do this and you shall live' " (Luke 10:25-28; see also Matthew 22:34-40).

In the Judaeo-Christian tradition of theology, a frequent discussion arose as to the priority to be given to each of the loves embraced in this commandment. Does the love of God come first or the love of neighbor? Certainly, priority must be given to the love of God: "This is the greatest and first commandment" (Matthew 22:38). Nor is this surprising, because to speak of God is to speak of the One who deserves to be loved above all things, the One who is supremely lovable.

But the second commandment demands a certain priority too, for it is "like the first," so intimately bound up with it that the two cannot be separated. Saint Alphonsus underlined the reason for this insistence on love of neighbor: "Why, therefore, must we love our neighbor? Because he is loved by God! We must love all whom God loves." Donald Goergen, a contemporary theologian, puts it this way: "Our God is the one who loves us, who loves men and women, who loves our neighbors.

No Christian response to God can be separated from loving those whom he loves" (*The Power of Love*).

In a very personal way, Jesus took "ownership" of this second commandment and deflected any possible misunderstanding of where he stood:

> This is my commandment:
> love one another
> as I have loved you. . . .
> The command I give you is this,
> that you love one another (John 15:12, 17).

Love in Action

I once heard a retreat master distinguish between what he called the "church virtue" of charity and the "street virtue." By the former he really meant a kind of pseudo-virtue: a warm feeling of universal love which might come over a person at a special moment of prayer in church but which, in effect, didn't demand anything of him or her. The "street virtue," on the other hand, was love in action: love in the ordinary relationships of daily life — charity in the family, in the neighborhood, at school, at work. It was the kind of charity described by Saint Paul in his famous hymn to love: "Love is patient; love is kind. Love is not jealous, it does not put on airs, it is not snobbish. Love is never rude, it is not self-seeking, it is not prone to anger; neither does it brood over injuries" (1 Corinthians 13:4-5).

Positive and Negative

Of the myriad ways open to the Christian for the practice of love, Saint Alphonsus emphasizes two positive and two negative approaches.

On the positive side, he first encourages the spirit of peace. He quotes Isaiah:

> Then the wolf shall be a guest of the lamb,
>   and the leopard shall lie down with the kid;

The calf and the young lion shall browse together,
   with a little child to guide them (Isaiah 11:6).

Commenting on that passage, Saint Alphonsus says: "By these words Isaiah wished to say that the followers of Jesus Christ, though from different nations and different climes and of unlike characters and temperaments, would nevertheless live peacefully together, for love would induce them to practice mutual forbearance."

Secondly, Alphonsus stresses almsgiving — the religious duty to help the poor and needy — not only out of our abundance but even, if necessary, out of what we consider essential for ourselves. He was fond of quoting the Old Testament Book of Tobit: "It is better to give alms than to store up gold; for almsgiving saves one from death and expiates every sin. Those who regularly give alms shall enjoy a full life . . . " (Tobit 12:8-9).

On the negative side, he cautions against rash judgment. "Dear Christian reader, if you desire to practice the beautiful virtue of charity, strive to reject every rash judgment, every distrust, and unfounded suspicion of your neighbor." He saw clearly that peace cannot blossom in a heart filled with suspicion, bitterness, or aversion.

In addition, he warns against uncharitable speech. With great insight he notes that "even among those who have vowed to strive after holiness there are many who cannot move their tongue without wounding someone." The true Christian will avoid calumny and detraction like plagues, and will try always to say only what is good of his or her neighbor.

Practical Suggestions

During April, as we try to grow in Christian love for neighbor, the following practical suggestions may come in handy:

First Week: Read and reflect on the First Letter of John. One of its themes is:
   This, remember, is the message

you heard from the beginning:
we should love one another (1 John 3:11).

Second Week: Examine our attitude toward peace: peace in our own families and communities and peace in the world. Do we earnestly desire peace? Are we trying to be peacemakers? (For many positive suggestions, read the 1983 pastoral letter of the American bishops, *The Challenge of Peace: God's Promise and Our Response.*)

Third Week: Conduct a searching inventory of our attitude toward and our practice of almsgiving. (To start the inventory, it might be helpful to make a list of all the exotic reasons why almsgiving is not possible in our circumstances!)

Fourth Week: Name one person with whom we find it hard to get along. Try to determine the reasons for this and plan a strategy of reconciliation with that person.

May

Poverty, the Enriching Gift

In the past twenty or so years, I have had the opportunity to travel widely on Church-related business. At workshops, retreats, marriage encounters, and the like, I have had the rare privilege of meeting and mingling with many marvelous Catholic people — bishops, priests, religious, laymen and laywomen both married and single. As I have reflected on my experiences, I have tried to pinpoint what, for me, are the most hopeful and encouraging "signs of the times" on the Catholic scene. Two especially stand out: (1) the fresh interest in, and practice of, prayer among Catholics of all ages and stages of life; and (2) the new awareness of and experiments in evangelical poverty.

There was a time, not too many years ago, when evangelical poverty was spoken of only occasionally — during retreats for men and women of religious communities, for example, or during meetings of what were then considered "fringe groups" of Catholics working with and for the poor. That is no longer the case. If you are attuned to dynamic developments in the

Church, if you read religious newspapers and journals, you will have no doubt that evangelical poverty is front and center on the Catholic stage today.

What Is Evangelical Poverty?

Like so many rich biblical concepts, evangelical poverty is hard to define in clear-cut terms. Over the centuries, however, there have been many and varied descriptions. One of the descriptions that brings together the chief elements of this virtue is that of Pope Paul VI. In 1971 Pope Paul wrote a simple but comprehensive message called "Evangelical Witness." Though primarily intended for men and women living the vowed life in religious communities, the basic thrust of this message applies to all disciples of Jesus, whatever their state in life or actual living conditions. One part of this message is on the meaning of evangelical poverty.

This virtue, wrote Pope Paul VI, is best grasped when one listens to "the cry of the poor." "You hear rising up, more pressing than ever, from their personal stress and collective misery, 'the cry of the poor.' " It is a cry that arose not only in biblical times, not only in times of primitive technology, but one that arises even in our affluent age. "In a world experiencing the full flood of development this persistence of poverty-stricken masses and individuals still constitutes a pressing call."

Jesus came to respond to this call. Of himself he says:

> The spirit of the Lord is upon me;
> therefore he has anointed me.
> He has sent me to bring glad tidings
> to the poor . . . (Luke 4:18).

Jesus even went so far as to identify himself with the poor (Matthew 25:35-40). Saint Alphonsus insisted that we would understand evangelical poverty only when we began to experience the generous love of Christ for us. One of his favorite texts was that of Saint Paul: "You are well acquainted with the favor shown you by our Lord Jesus Christ: how for your sake he made himself poor though he was rich, so that you might become rich by his poverty" (2 Corinthians 8:9).

Like Master, like disciple! As disciples of Jesus we are called to share his views on the true place of material possessions in our lives and on the danger of riches. "Remember, where your treasure is, there your heart is also. . . . No man can serve two masters. He will either hate one and love the other or be attentive to one and despise the other. You cannot give yourself to God and money" (Matthew 6:21, 24). For the disciple of Christ today, said Pope Paul, the cry of the poor "constitutes a pressing call for a conversion of mind and heart."

"An Echo in Your Lives"

As with any virtue, so with evangelical poverty: the challenge is to put it into practice! Or, in Pope Paul's words, "How will the cry of the poor find an echo in your lives?" He answers this question by providing several guidelines:

First, the cry of the poor must bar us "from whatever would be a compromise with any form of social injustice." From hard experience we know that social injustice is all around us, and we know how easy it is to compromise with it! Among other things, social injustice certainly includes: dishonest business practices; racial, ethnic, and sexual discrimination; disregard for the rights of workers and the rights of employers; neglectful, and even harsh, treatment of the truly poor and needy. Who among us has not compromised with these injustices?

Second, the cry of the poor must keep us from being "carried away by an uncurbed seeking of our own ease" and from being "enticed by the security of possessions, knowledge and power." Saint Alphonsus was absolutely convinced that evangelical poverty — "poverty of spirit and a spirit of poverty" — demanded detachment of the heart from material possessions and worldly power. He encouraged people to gain perspective by meditating on death as "the day of loss" when riches and possessions would be no more.

Third, the cry of the poor must encourage us to "fraternal sharing with our needy brothers and sisters." Such sharing is an imperative of evangelical poverty. It is a sharing that calls for generosity and a firm trust in the Lord. It is related to what Michael Foley has called the "poverty of enough." The truth is that many of us have enough and more than enough. The trouble is, writes Foley, "our wants are measured not against basic human needs but against standards set in the pages of *Better Homes and Gardens* and *Outdoor Living*. Our problem with poverty is not so much a fear of false economy as our own false expectations. It is not that we value quality but that we worship fashion. Above all, we exalt economic abundance above both our own freedom and the needs of others" (*Sojourners*, September, 1983).

Practical Suggestions

During the month of May we might try to deepen our appreciation of and commitment to evangelical poverty in these ways:

First Week: Read and reflect on the following passages from the Gospel of Matthew: 5:1-12 on the Beatitudes; 6:19-34 on true riches; 19:16-30 on the danger of riches; 25:31-45 on the Final Judgment.

Second Week: Carefully examine our consciences on issues of social justice. Do our values and viewpoints reflect those of the Christian tradition and the teaching of the Church? (See the bibliography at the end of this booklet for reading suggestions.)

Third Week: Make a will; or review the one already made. Does it reflect well-ordered charity toward our loved ones, especially dependents? Is there any place in it for the works of social justice, for sharing with the needy, for building the Kingdom of God on earth? If not, why not?

Fourth Week: Make a definite plan and commitment to share something real this week — food, clothing, shelter, a sum of money — with someone truly in need.

June

Chastity, the Personal Gift

Of all the words that have passed from the Catholic lexicon in recent years, none seems to have passed so quickly and completely as the word *chastity*. There are some Catholics, I know, who do not mourn its passing. For them the word conjured up a cramped and restrictive view of human sexuality, a nit-picking negativism that overshadowed the positive meaning of sex as love-giving and life-giving. While not abandoning Christian values in relationship to sex, these people seem convinced that "chastity" is a word that belongs to another age.

Whatever may be said about the word, the need for some moderation and control of sexual drives is beyond dispute. The opposite of chastity is lust. Lust is the disordered and unrestrained seeking of sexual pleasure; it creates the dank and depressing environment of sexual exploitation. Lust gives birth to many offspring, including pornography, prostitution, impersonal perversions of all kinds. While chastity may indeed be demanding and challenging, it is certainly more authentically human than its opposite.

For the Christian, moreover, chastity is concerned not only with moderation of sexual pleasure, it is intimately related to love and holiness: "It is God's will that you grow in holiness: that you abstain from immorality, each of you guarding his member in sanctity and honor, not in passionate desire as do the Gentiles who know not God . . . " (1 Thessalonians 4:3-5). "Be imitators of God as his dear children. Follow the way of love, even as Christ loved you. . . . As for lewd conduct or promiscuousness or lust of any sort, let them not even be mentioned among you; your holiness forbids this" (Ephesians 5:1-4).

The Foundations of Chastity

As a soaring bridge relies for its strength on pilings set deep in the riverbed, so does chastity rest on several fundamental Christian beliefs.

The first of these basic beliefs is that sex is a *good gift* of God to men and women.

> Then God said: 'Let us make man in our image, after our likeness' . . .
> God created man in his image;
> in the divine image he created him;
> male and female he created them. . . .
> God looked at everything he had made, and he found it very good . . . (Genesis 1:26-27, 31).

The recurrent heresy that sex is evil and one of God's mistakes must be rejected.

The second basic belief is that sex is an *important gift*. It is important both for the individual person and for the family; it is one of the pillars upon which society stands. Because it is important, Christians (unlike the writers of so many movie and TV scripts) have always been serious about it. With great insight, James Hanigan points out: "While sex may indeed be fun, and often even funny, it is not a matter for mere jest and amusement. . . . For ultimately sex and sexuality are only abstractions. The concrete reality is the sexed human being, male or female, made in the image and likeness of God. To trivialize sex, to make it a subject of jest or of little importance, is to cheapen the human person" (*What Are They Saying About Sexual Morality?*).

The third fundamental belief is that God has built into human sexuality certain intrinsic meanings that cannot be erased or ignored. According to Catholic teaching, these meanings are articulated in the Church by the Holy Father and the bishops in communion with him. Guided by the Holy Spirit, they have the pastoral duty to express the teaching of Christ on moral questions and matters of belief.

Though we cannot present all of this teaching in this brief chapter, we can at least call attention to the most basic principles of sexual morality as expressed by the magisterium of the Church.

1. The Christian tradition holds the sexual union between husband and wife in high honor. It is indeed a special expression of their covenanted love, which mirrors God's love for his people and Christ's love for the Church. In the words of Vatican II, "Married love is uniquely expressed and perfected by the exercise of the acts proper to marriage. Hence the acts in marriage by which the intimate and chaste union of the spouses takes place are noble and honorable; the truly human performance of these acts fosters the self-giving they signify and enriches the spouses in joy and gratitude" (*Church in the Modern World*, 49). But, where marriage does not exist, where there is no stable community of life and love, where there is no self-giving commitment, sexual union is morally wrong.

2. In the sexual union between husband and wife there is an inseparable connection between the unitive (love-giving) and the procreative (life-giving) meanings of sexual intercourse. Spouses, on their own initiative, are not morally justified in separating these two meanings. For this reason, artificial contraception is considered morally wrong.

3. The marriage covenant calls for a sexual love that is faithful and exclusive — in good times and in bad, in sickness

and in health. Adultery is a direct attack on this faithful and exclusive love. By adultery the truth of sexual love in marriage is betrayed.

Concupiscence and Control

The fourth fundamental belief of the Church is that concupiscence is real and in need of control. Concupiscence, a result of original sin, means that the desires of the flesh are not automatically subject to reason and grace. "The lust of the flesh," as Pope John Paul II has written, "is a permanent element of man's fallen nature." Because of concupiscence, there is a tendency for men and women to turn true, other-centered sexual love into a mere self-centered satisfaction.

Concupiscence needs control. Evelyn Duvall uses this apt analogy: When properly harnessed, electricity can bring many comforts into our homes; left unleashed, as lightning, it can destroy our homes. The saints are unanimous in directing us to cultivate the virtue of chastity so that we will be able to keep concupiscence under the control of reason and grace. They echo Saint Paul who proclaimed, "The law of the spirit, the spirit of life in Christ Jesus, has freed you from the law of sin and death" (Romans 8:2), and who encouraged his people not to be discouraged by the struggle against "the wiles of the devil," but to stand firm in prayer and mortification.

Saint Alphonsus believed that the subtlest dangers in regard to chastity were "occasions of sin." In moral theology, the treatise on "occasions of sin" can be quite complicated. Briefly, Saint Alphonsus is referring here to occasions of sin that are voluntary (that is, of our own choosing and therefore easily avoidable) and proximate (that is, those that frequently lead a person into sin). He describes the plight of sincere Christian men and women who really want to lead chaste lives. They pray; they make good resolutions; but often enough they wind up back in the sexual morass they wanted to escape. Why is this? His answer: because they voluntarily placed themselves into proximate occasions of sin. Such occasions of sin, he said, were like steel nets which ensnared and pressured the person until he or she gave in. He believed that avoiding such occasions of sin was one of the most practical ways of gaining moral freedom and of growing in chastity.

Practical Suggestions

To cultivate the virtue of chastity during this month of June, the following suggestions may be helpful:

First Week: Read and pray over these Scripture passages: Genesis 1, 2, and 3; Matthew 19:1-15; John 8:1-11; Ephesians 5.

Second Week: Keep a running list of ways in which sex is trivialized in our society. At the end of the week, reflect on this list and ask ourselves how we personally are influenced by these ways.

Third Week: Write a letter to an imaginary teenager, stating our most basic values about human sexuality and sexual behavior, explaining why we hold these values and what difficulties we experience in making them a part of our lives.

Fourth Week: Is there a particular free and proximate occasion of unchastity into which I frequently place myself? What would be a good strategy for dealing with this in a realistic way?

July

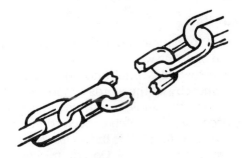

Obedience, the Liberating Gift

Some adult Christians seem to think that the virtue of obedience, like Santa Claus and the Easter bunny, is "for the children." To be sure, obedience is a key virtue of childhood. It acknowledges that the growing child needs help and direction, and it is part of the "honor" due to one's parents. When we ourselves become adults, however, the duty to obey our parents ceases (though the duty to honor and respect them lasts all the days of our lives).

Does it follow, then, that the virtue of obedience has no place in the life of an adult? Quite the contrary! From one point of view, obedience is the most basic of all the Christian virtues. Like the air we breathe, obedience is an essential part of our total spiritual environment. Though we may not be conscious of it at all times, it pervades our lives and is a constant in our response to God.

Since this claim may seem exaggerated, I would like in these few pages to indicate why the Christian tradition believes it to be true. There is not enough space to paint in all the details, but even this broad sketch will show how magnificent the Christian vision is. The key to the vision is the full meaning of law. Law may be understood in many ways. Let's look at some of them.

The Eternal Law

The most profound meaning of law is the eternal law of God: that is, the plan of divine wisdom insofar as it directs all activity and all change toward a final end. This is the eternal and universal law whereby, in the words of Vatican II, "God orders, directs and governs the whole world and the ways of the human community according to a plan conceived in his wisdom and love" (*Religious Liberty,* 3). It is the source of all other law and the foundation of all authority. God promulgates this eternal law both in creation (the natural law) and in revelation (divine positive law).

All creatures are called to carry out this eternal law of God. Irrational creatures carry it out necessarily, guided by natural forces. The tree gives glory to God by being a tree! Rational creatures, made in God's image, are expected to carry it out intelligently and voluntarily.

The Natural Law

That brings us to the natural law. By this we mean the sharing of the rational creature in the eternal law of God. For, as Vatican II expresses it, "God has enabled man to participate in this law of his so that, under the gentle disposition of divine providence, many may be able to arrive at a deeper and deeper knowledge of unchangeable truth" (*Religious Liberty,* 3). God in his wisdom created human nature for a purpose. He endowed men and women with a natural tendency or drive toward that purpose. This natural law, as Saint Paul describes it, is an inner law; it is "written in their hearts" (Romans 2:15).

When men and women act in accordance with human nature and its inherent characteristics and propensities, they act in accordance with the natural law and the eternal law of God. They perceive general truths such as "Good must be done; evil must be avoided." Then they move to basic moral principles, such as "Human life is inviolable" or "Basic human rights must be respected." Over the centuries, as men and women have reflected upon their own nature and their relationships in society, they have arrived at even more particular moral norms that are almost universally agreed upon, such as: It is wrong to murder, to steal, to commit adultery.

The Divine Positive Law

The eternal law of God is manifested in a fuller and clearer way through divine revelation. God manifested his will through "the law and the prophets" in the Old Testament and "in this, the final age, he has spoken to us through his Son [Jesus]" (Hebrews 1:2). In some cases, God reaffirms and clarifies the basics of natural law (for example, in the Ten Commandments). In other cases, he calls us far beyond the natural law — for example, in the teaching of Jesus on the new Law of Love.

Human Law

Finally, there is human law. This may be either civil law or Church law. Civil law may be defined as an ordinance of reason promulgated by authority for the common good. Civil authority of some kind is necessary to bring about order in society and to work for the benefit of all the citizens. True civil authority is from God, "for there is no authority except from God, and all authority that exists is established by God" (Romans 13:1).

Church law flows from the power Christ gave to his Church to bind or loose. "He who hears you, hears me" (Luke 10:16). This authority is exercised by the pope and ecumenical councils for the entire Church and by bishops for their dioceses. The Code of Canon Law (most recently revised in 1983) contains the laws of the Holy See.

The Virtue of Obedience

In light of all this, we can say that the virtue of obedience is the moral virtue which inclines the Christian to submit to the law of God in all of its manifestations. God alone is the ultimate source of all law. Obedience is a positive response not merely to civil decrees or ecclesiastical statutes but to the authority of God himself. In striving to know and observe the natural law, in listening to and obeying the law of God as expressed in Sacred Scripture, in keeping the laws of the Church and the just laws of society — the Christian person is constantly rendering obedience to God himself!

It goes without saying that our obedience to God must be absolute and complete. But our obedience to human authority is limited; if human authority opposes the authority of God and commands something immoral or sinful, then "better for us to obey God than men!" (Acts 5:29)

For the Christian, obedience is intimately linked to love. It is a very practical way of showing love, as Jesus himself points out:

> You will live in my love
> if you keep my commandments,
> even as I have kept my Father's commandments,
> and live in his love (John 15:10).

In truth, the whole life of Jesus is a shining example of obedience. He came not to do his own will but the will of the Father (John 5:30). In his suffering and death he submitted obediently to the Father. "Son though he was, he learned obedience from what he suffered; and when perfected, he became the source of eternal salvation for all who obey him . . . " (Hebrews 5:8-9).

In this context, Thomas Merton often pointed out that Christian obedience is not slavery or servitude, as so many people seem to think, but a loving response to Jesus. "The Christian is not merely one who keeps the rules imposed on him by the Church. True, he keeps the commandments of God as well as the laws of the Church — but his reason for doing so is not to be looked for in any power of legal decrees: it is found in Christ: Jesus himself, living in us by his spirit, is our rule of life" (*New Seeds of Contemplation*).

Practical Suggestions

In trying to grow in the virtue of obedience during July, the following steps may be helpful to us:

First Week: Read and pray over the Gospel of John, chapters 13-17, with this question in mind: What do these passages tell us about the obedience of Jesus?

Second Week: Spell out for ourselves the specific ways in which obedience is required of us at this time of our lives; we might think of family, job, neighborhood, nation.

Third Week: Examine any negative feelings we may have about the moral teaching of Jesus or the laws of the Church. Where do these negative feelings come from? Are these negative feelings in some way related to a false understanding of obedience?

Fourth Week: Make a list of any laws of our society that we are opposed to. After each, state the reason why we are opposed to them. In light of our reasons, are we justified in disobeying them?

August

Humility, the Honest Gift

Many years ago, when I was in college, I attended a seminar on sales techniques. I don't remember many details, but I do remember the message of the keynote speaker. It contained most of the familiar clichés: You must sell yourself; you must be aggressive; you must not let the customer off the hook. One sentence especially struck me: "For a salesman," he said, "humility is a great handicap."

I suspect that many people, whether salespersons or not, would endorse that view. Humility is not one of the all-time favorite virtues of modern Christians. By and large, is it not considered a negative virtue rather than a positive one, a repressive virtue rather than a liberating one?

Yet, humility holds a central place in the life and teaching of Jesus. He called special attention to it when he issued his personal invitation: ". . . Learn from me, for I am gentle and humble of heart" (Matthew 11:29). And Saint Paul's profound description of the spirit of Jesus underlines humility:

> Though he was in the form of God,
>   he did not deem equality with God
>   something to be grasped at.
> Rather, he emptied himself
>   and took the form of a slave,
>   being born in the likeness of men.
> He was known to be of human estate,
>   and it was thus that he humbled himself,
>   obediently accepting even death,
>   death on a cross! (Philippians 2:6-8)

This emphasis was not lost on the early Christian community. The Fathers of the Church, almost without exception, call attention to the virtue of humility. "Christian thought and practice," writes Father Bernard Häring, "has always looked upon it as a fundamental virtue serving as the foundation of the whole edifice of Christian virtue" (*The Law of Christ*).

Humility Is Truth

Though it is not possible to summarize here all that the Christian tradition says about humility, it will be worthwhile to zero in on a basic understanding of it. Such an understanding is provided by the great Saint Teresa of Avila: "Humility is truth." That is an excellent definition, provided, of course, that we understand it. To understand it, we have to break it into two parts. Humility is truth, to be sure, but truth in self-understanding and truth in action.

Truth in self-understanding is the core of humility. It means that we have a real awareness of our human condition as creatures of God. It means that we are convinced of this most basic truth about ourselves: that God is our Creator and the Source of all our gifts. "For the God who made the world and all that is in it, the Lord of heaven and earth, does not dwell in sanctuaries made by human hands; nor does he receive man's service as if he were in need of it. Rather, it is he who gives to all life and breath and everything else. . . . In him we live and move and have our being . . . " (Acts 17:24-28).

The most basic truth about ourselves is that every gift and talent we have comes to us from the creative hand of God. Truth in self-knowledge asks only that we remember this. Humility does not demand that we deny the gifts and talents we have. It demands only that we acknowledge where they came from. The theme song of the humble person could well be: "Who confers any distinction on you? Name something you have that you have not received. If, then, you have received it, why are you boasting as if it were your own?" (1 Corinthians 4:7)

Saint Alphonsus expressed this same truth by way of a delightful analogy. "A proud person is like a balloon filled with air, which appears great, but whose greatness, in reality, is nothing more than a little air which is lost as soon as the balloon is opened. He who loves God is not deceived by his own qualities because he knows that whatever he possesses is a gift of God, that without God he possesses only nothingness."

Truth in Action

Truth in action implies that our basic convictions about ourselves and our abilities and talents (as outlined above) affect our manner, our speech, our association with others. Our entire manner will indicate that whatever talents we have are gifts of God. That is the truth, and we are happy to live in accord with it! We do not, therefore, put on airs or belittle others. We don't have to. We know the truth, and the truth sets us free.

Freedom is indeed one of the fruits of humility: freedom from the tyranny of false images, from the petty conflicts of jealousy and envy, from the vain struggle to be what we are not. Dom Hubert Van Zeller expresses this well: "The humble can afford to be supremely unconcerned about many of the things which upset the proud. The humble man does not bother about what others are saying of him, does not waste time in trying to create an impression, does not scheme for positions, does not suspect other peoples' motives, does not worry when he cannot get what he wants, does not go in for spite or a desire for revenge. In fact the humble man is spared a good deal."

Peace, too, is a fruit of humility. Inner peace comes when fear is overcome. Humility teaches us that we have nothing to fear, that God loves us and cares about us and has gifted us. Thomas Merton remarks that "a humble man is not afraid of failure. In fact, he is not afraid of anything, even of himself, since perfect humility implies confidence in the power of God, before whom no other power has any meaning and for whom there is no such thing as an obstacle."

Yet, even though humility holds out a promise of freedom and peace, it is hard to commit ourselves to it. In an aggressive and competitive culture like our own, are we not secretly afraid that others will take advantage of us or walk all over us? What we forget, of course, is that humility gives us a whole new perspective on life. It takes the sting out of many of the things that used to give us ulcers. Even in a culture like ours, it is worth a try!

Practical Suggestions

During August, as we try to nourish the virtue of humility, the following suggestions may be helpful:

First Week: Pray over this litany of humility of Abbot Marmion: *(The response is:* Deliver me, O Jesus!*)*

From the inordinate desire of being . . .
   esteemed
   praised
   honored
   approved

From the inordinate fear of being . . .
   humbled
   rebuked
   forgotten
   insulted

Second Week: Examine our lives under the light of these questions: Do I really acknowledge my true relationship with God as Creator and Giver of all gifts? Does this have a real impact on my behavior?

Third Week: Write out examples, drawn from our own experience, of the difference between true humility and false humility. Give the reasons for our choices.

Fourth Week: Think of a person who has impressed us as being truly humble. What precisely are the qualities that attract us to such a person?

September

Mortification, the Renewing Gift

If you are a thoroughly modern Millie (or Willie), you may never have heard the word *mortification* as used in the Christian tradition of spirituality. It certainly has not reached the top of the charts in the modern Church. On the other hand, if you are one of those Catholics who grew up with words like *mortification, detachment,* and *self-denial,* you may wonder if they still have a place in the Christian life.

It is beyond dispute that the spiritual writings of the saints — of every age and culture — are full of explanations and examples of mortification. How important is their teaching? Does it still apply? Since mortification is our "virtue of the month" for September, let's briefly examine these and other questions.

What Does Mortification Mean?

The word *mortification* has its roots in the Latin word *mors,* which means death. In English, mortification is sometimes used to refer to a feeling of humiliation or embarrassment, as in "I was mortified when I forgot my speech . . . or when I spilled my soup at the boss's party." In a deeper sense, however, it refers to the Christian ideal of "dying to self" through the deliberate restraint of unruly passions and appetites. It refers to the struggle against one's evil inclinations so as to bring them into conformity with the will of God.

Like a key to a lock, the idea of Christian mortification is intimately related to the teaching of Jesus. "Jesus said to all: 'Whoever wishes to be my follower must deny his very self, take up his cross each day, and follow in my steps. Whoever would save his life will lose it, and whoever loses his life for my sake will save it' " (Luke 9:23-24). "He who seeks only himself brings himself to ruin, whereas he who brings himself to nought for me discovers who he is" (Matthew 10:39).

Saint Paul sounded this same note: "Those who belong to Christ Jesus have crucified their flesh with its passions and desires" (Galatians 5:24). And he speaks in dire terms of those who "go about in a way which shows them to be enemies of the cross of Christ . . . Such as these will end in disaster. Their god is their belly and their glory is in their shame. I am talking about those who are set upon the things of this world" (Philippians 3:18-19).

Why Mortification?

To modern ears this emphasis on self-denial, this negative renunciation of passions and desires, raises troubling questions. Have not the spiritual leaders of our times (including the Fathers of Vatican Council II) been emphasizing the positive values of creation and of the human person, including the body and the emotions? "God doesn't make junk" is a slogan that contains a lot of wisdom. Even Pope John Paul II has often emphasized the importance of true Christian self-love and the basic value of the human emotions. Isn't there a contradiction between what we believe now about the goodness of ourselves and what we are told about "dying to self"?

A clue to this apparent contradiction can be found only in a balanced Christian understanding of human nature. In effect, human nature is neither all good nor all bad; it is a delicate balance of both. No one has struggled to express this balance more truthfully than Saint Paul, the mystic and the missionary of the early Church. Like an artist straining to communicate the truth, Paul uses a number of images and comparisons to describe human nature.

He speaks, for example, of the war between "the flesh" and "the spirit" — or, as some translations have it, between "the spiritual self" and "the unspiritual self." It should be noted that in Saint Paul the term *flesh* refers not merely to the human body or to sexual concupiscence but, rather, to the state of unredeemed human nature in its earthly or secular condition. "Those who live according to the flesh are intent on the things of the flesh, those who live according to the spirit, on those of the spirit. The tendency of the flesh is toward death but that of the spirit toward life and peace. The flesh in its tendency is at enmity with God; it is not subject to God's law. . . . If you live according to the flesh, you will die; but if by the spirit you put to death the evil deeds of the body, you will live" (Romans 8:5-13).

Paul also contrasts "the old self" and "the new self," insisting that "you must lay aside your former way of life and the old self which deteriorates through illusion and desire, and acquire a fresh, spiritual way of thinking" (Ephesians 4:22-23). Changing the image, he describes the same reality in terms of light and darkness. "There was a time when you were darkness, but now you are light in the Lord. Well, then, live as children of light. . . . Take no part in vain deeds done in darkness; rather, condemn them" (Ephesians 5:8-11).

Through the ages the saints, in their various ways, have simply repeated what Saint Paul has described. Mortification is necessary to keep under control the unspiritual, unregenerated, dark, selfish elements of human nature. In this sense, it is a very negative virtue. But its purpose is positive: to nourish the spiritual, renewed, bright side of human nature that makes us more like Christ.

Kinds of Mortification

While it is not possible to attempt a complete review of the teaching of the saints on mortification, I would like to underscore two important points made by Saint Alphonsus Liguori. First, he makes a distinction between external mortification and internal mortification; and second, between self-chosen mortifications and those sent by God. A word about each.

External mortification refers to the discipline of the senses, such as fasting, abstinence, control of the tongue, modesty of the eyes. It is important for the Christian, especially when necessary to avoid sin or when imposed by the law of the Church, as in the case of Lenten fast and abstinence.

Internal mortification refers to "discipline of the heart," control over our errant passions and emotions. According to Saint Alphonsus, this kind of mortification is much more important . . . and also much less common. He describes Christians who engage in fasting and other corporal austerities but who "make no effort to overcome certain passions, for example, certain resentments, aversions, curiosity, and dangerous attachments." Such Christians, he feels, will not make much real progress in holiness!

Concerning the choosing of mortifications, Saint Alphonsus encouraged people to select practices that would be helpful to them in their concrete circumstances. Yet, he insisted that the crosses and hardships that came to us from the Lord and from living the Christian life were more sanctifying: patience in time of sickness or old age, for example, courage in dealing with personality conflicts or family problems, fortitude in difficult tasks. Bearing these crosses with a loving spirit would bring us close to Christ!

Practical Suggestions

First Week: Read and pray over Romans, chapters 1-8.

Second Week: Take an honest inventory of the "unspiritual, unregenerated, dark, selfish elements" that we see in ourselves here and now.

Third Week: Question ourselves about external mortification: How do I really feel about this traditional aspect of Christian life? Is there a need for this in my life at this time? How should I go about it?

Fourth Week: Question ourselves about internal mortification. Am I lacking something here? What would be a fruitful approach for me at this time?

October

Recollection, the Enlightening Gift

According to the plan of Saint Alphonsus, which we have been following in this booklet, the virtue for the month of October is recollection. "What kind of a virtue is that?" you may ask. "I never heard of it before!" In truth, as Saint Alphonsus himself points out, it is really not a specific virtue like obedience or humility but, rather, a stimulus to the practice of all the other Christian virtues. Moreover, the idea behind it becomes a little clearer when we give it its full title: the recollection of the presence of God.

Perfect union with God is the ultimate hope of the Christian. According to Catholic teaching, eternal happiness consists precisely in the face-to-face vision of God. In heaven "we shall be like him, for we shall see him as he is" (1 John 3:2), and we shall be enthralled by his beauty and lovableness. "Now we see indistinctly, as in a mirror; then we shall see face to face. My knowledge is imperfect now; then I shall know even as I am known" (1 Corinthians 13:12).

Though we must wait for this perfect union, we have even now the privilege and the responsibility of cultivating a real union with God through love. This is, in fact, the whole point of living a spiritual life, a life of prayer, a life of Christian virtue. Saint Alphonsus reminds us that just as human love is strengthened by the presence of the beloved, so too our love for God is strengthened by being aware of his presence. "The more we walk in the presence of God the better we recognize his beautiful qualities that increase and strengthen his love in our hearts."

Walking in the Presence of God

In characteristic fashion, Saint Alphonsus not only encourages us to focus on the presence of God but also shows us how we might go about it. He offers four "means of walking in God's presence" and suggests that we use the ones that are most helpful to us. Here, in abbreviated form, are the four.

1. "A good means of walking in God's presence is to picture our Lord as present to us wherever we happen to be." It is helpful — especially for young people — to think of Jesus as an infant in Bethlehem, as a carpenter's apprentice in Nazareth, as a well-loved preacher in Galilee, as a man of sorrows in his suffering and death on Calvary. In this way, we can more easily relate his life to our own.

2. "Another and better means of walking in the presence of God is based on the truths of holy faith." Faith tells us that God is everywhere and that he sustains us in being: "For the God who made the world and all that is in it, the Lord of heaven and earth, does not dwell in sanctuaries made by human hands; nor does he receive man's service as if he were in need of it. Rather, it is he who gives to all life and breath and everything else . . . he is not really far from any one of us" (Acts 17:24-27). From time to time through the day, we need simply advert to the presence of God, making a small act of faith such as: "My God, I believe that you are lovingly present here and now."

3. "Still another beautiful practice is seeing God in his creatures." The created universe — the rising of the sun, the magnificence of a mountain, the majesty of a river, the brilliance of a star — speaks to us of the beauty of God. Human

beings speak even more eloquently of him. The wise or beautiful or holy persons we meet actually reflect the wisdom, the beauty, the holiness of God. "Let us return thanks to God for permitting his creatures to share in his holy attributes."

4. "The most perfect method of keeping alive the thought of God's presence consists in beholding God within our very selves." Surely one of the most precious of all Christian truths is that God dwells within those who love him!

> Anyone who loves me
> will be true to my word,
> and my Father will love him;
> we will come to him
> and make our dwelling place with him (John 14:23).

To cultivate an awareness of this special presence of God is a giant step on the road to holiness.

The Environment of Silence

Keeping alive the vivid recollection of God's presence is not easy. Most of us are surrounded by disturbances and distractions of all kinds. For this reason, Saint Alphonsus — and all the other masters of the spiritual life — insists that we must try to create an environment of silence and solitude. Though it may seem anti-American to say it, noise tends to split and wound the human spirit; silence tends to heal and refresh it. Certainly, without some measure of silence and solitude, we can easily ignore the presence of God. "For every one who wishes to hear what is true and real," writes Ladislaus Boros, S.J., "every voice must for once be still. Silence, however, is not merely the absence of speech. . . . It is a depth, a fullness, a peaceful flow of hidden life" (*God Is with Us*).

Perhaps the first reaction of the average lay person to this emphasis on silence and solitude would be something like this: "Are you kidding? That may work in monasteries and convents, but not where I live or work!" Saint Alphonsus must have heard this objection, too, because he directly confronts it when he says: "To find this refreshing solitude it is not necessary to withdraw into a desert or live in a cave; you can find it in your home and in the midst of your family." I know a number of people, even parents of small children, who have established a "quiet corner" in their house or apartment. Here, each morning and evening, they take time to be silent, to be conscious of God's presence, to be renewed in spirit.

But the spirit of recollection ought not be confined to set times and places. It should become part of the rhythm of daily life. Thus, we can lovingly attend to God's presence — as we begin a new chore, wait at the check-out counter, stop for a traffic light, walk from one office or classroom to another. In such simple ways we become attuned, as was the psalmist, to the ever-present God:

O LORD, you have probed me and you know me;
   you know when I sit and when I stand;
   you understand my thoughts from afar.
My journeys and my rest you scrutinize,
   with all my ways you are familiar (Psalm 139:1-3).

Practical Suggestions

As we concentrate this month on developing a spirit of recollection, the following steps may be helpful:

First Week: Prayerfully reflect on these Psalms: Psalm 63 (Longing for God); Psalm 104 (God's creative wisdom and power); Psalm 139 (The presence of God).

Second Week: Write out in our own words, for the benefit of someone who has never heard of recollection, a practical explanation of what it means to us.

Third Week: Make a list of times in a typical day when a few moments of recollection would be both workable and helpful; experiment this week with these times.

Fourth Week: Decide to create in our house or apartment a "quiet corner" where, as Thomas Merton expressed it, "your mind can be idle, and forget its concerns, descend into silence, and worship the Father in secret."

November

Prayer, the Unifying Gift

Prayer is the heart of the practical plan of spirituality presented by Saint Alphonsus Liguori. As the heart pumps life-giving blood to all parts of the body, so prayer enlivens the whole Christian life. Without it, spiritual growth is impossible. Because he considered prayer so essential to Christian living, Saint Alphonsus wrote several books entirely dedicated to it. Of all his books (more than one hundred), he considered his treatises on prayer the most significant for the average person.

In these few pages we cannot do justice to the rich teaching of Saint Alphonsus on the topic of prayer. We can touch only the highlights: namely, his emphasis on the Eucharist, on meditation, and on the prayer of petition.

The Worship of God

With the great Saint Thomas Aquinas, Saint Alphonsus teaches that the virtue of religion, or the worship of God, holds first place in the lineup of moral virtues. This is so because "it is occupied more with God and leads us nearer to him than the other virtues." Every Christian, therefore, should make the worship of God his or her highest priority.

How to do this? "The easiest means — a means that we can employ at all times and in all places — is found in prayer. Whether it be the prayer of praise and thanksgiving or petition or atonement, we are worshiping God! Every prayer is a humble acknowledgment of the greatness or goodness or faithfulness or loving kindness of God."

The Holy Eucharist

The greatest prayer of praise and thanksgiving is the celebration of the sacrifice and sacrament of the Eucharist. It is the summit of worship and the source of life in the Church: "the most venerable sacrament . . . in which Christ the Lord is contained, offered and received, and by which the Church continually lives and grows" (Code of Canon Law, 897).

Saint Alphonsus taught that the best way to join in the celebration of the Eucharist was by making our own the fundamental purposes for which it was instituted. He encouraged Catholics to attend Mass, therefore, with great attention to these purposes: "First, to honor and glorify God. Secondly, to give thanks to him for all of his gifts and benefits. Thirdly, to make satisfaction for our own sins and the sins of others. Fourthly, to obtain the many graces which we need." Even in our day when liturgical theology is so well developed, it would be difficult to find a better short summary of the spirit that should mark our celebration of the Eucharist!

Another characteristic emphasis of Saint Alphonsus was on "visiting the Blessed Sacrament." Even outside of Mass, as the Church professes, the Eucharist should be reverenced with the greatest devotion. In his world-famous *Visits to the Blessed Sacrament,* Saint Alphonsus offers a wide variety of sentiments and prayers for this devotion. The basic thrust is captured in this sentence: "Let us, then, draw near to Jesus with great confidence and affection; let us unite ourselves to him, and let us ask him for graces."

Meditation

It would be hard to exaggerate the importance Saint Alphonsus placed on meditation: that is, the wordless, interior reflection on and response to the revealed Word of God. He used a number of images to explain its importance. He saw it, for example, as a kind of spiritual vision. "The truths of faith are spiritual realities; they cannot be seen with the bodily eyes, but only with the eyes of the soul, that is to say, by reflection or meditation." Without meditation, he said, we could only stumble around in the dark.

He compared meditation to fire. "Meditation affects the soul as fire does iron. If iron is cold, it is very hard and cannot be molded without great difficulty. But put it in fire, and at once it softens and easily yields to the efforts of the blacksmith.... So too our hearts are often hard and obstinate. But under the influence of grace which we receive in meditation, our hearts grow pliable and docile and can be molded by our Lord and Master."

Our hearts will more readily respond to God in silent, interior, reflective prayer than in any other way. If we are serious about growth in the Christian life, therefore, we must commit ourselves to this kind of prayer. Saint Alphonsus insisted that every person set aside at least fifteen minutes a day for meditation. Only the gravest emergency should be allowed to interfere with that prayer time. Those who would so commit themselves would soon find themselves, he said, listening to the Word of God with joy and responding to it with love!

Prayer of Petition

Some teachers and preachers at the time of Saint Alphonsus tended to downgrade the prayer of petition. They implied that it was not "pure" enough, not sufficiently "elevated" for holy people. Saint Alphonsus rejected their viewpoint. He insisted that we listen, rather, to the teaching of Jesus. "Ask, and you will receive. Seek, and you will find. Knock, and it will be opened to you" (Matthew 7:7). Or again:

> I give you my assurance,
>   whatever you ask the Father,
>   he will give you in my name (John 16:23).

If we are tempted to think that the saints became holy by some magical formula not available to the rest of humankind, we are wrong. In the opinion of Saint Alphonsus, the saints became holy because they prayed! "All the graces by means of which they have become saints were received by them in answer to their prayers." That very same way of prayer is open to us also. "We need humility; let us ask for it and we shall be humble. We need patience under tribulation; let us ask for it and we shall be patient. Divine love is what we desire; let us ask for it and we shall obtain it."

One of the most insightful and consoling points of theology developed by Saint Alphonsus is that God grants to all men and women, even the most hardhearted and sinful, the grace to pray! He puts it this way: "Taking for granted that prayer is necessary for gaining eternal life, we should also take for granted that everyone has sufficient aid from God to enable him to pray. And by prayer he can obtain all other graces necessary to persevere in keeping the commandments and so gain eternal life."

Practical Suggestions

As we try to enrich our life of prayer during this month of November, the following suggestions may prove helpful:

First Week: Prayerfully meditate on the following passages from the Gospel of Luke: 11:1-13, 18:1-14, 22:39-46.

Second Week: Ask ourselves: Is the Eucharistic liturgy the highpoint of our prayer life? What do we like most about it as we experience it? What do we like least? What are some steps we can take to enhance our participation?

Third Week: Make a resolution to set aside at least fifteen minutes a day for meditative and reflective prayer. Nail down the details this week so that the resolution will be practical.

Fourth Week: Examine and share with another person (for example, spiritual director or personal friend) our attitudes toward the prayer of petition. Do we have sufficient confidence in the promises of Jesus?

December

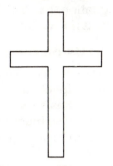

Love of the Cross, the Redemptive Gift

As we come now to the end of the year and the last of "the monthly virtues" as proposed by Saint Alphonsus Liguori, I'm sorry I have to be the bearer of bad tidings! At this time of year when Christmas lights twinkle on Main Street and Christmas music floats from every door, I must warn you that the virtue for December does not have a Christmasy ring to it! At first glance, it seems to have a Good Friday ring to it. It is called: Love of the Cross.

On second thought, however, Saint Alphonsus would probably not agree that a Christmas note is lacking in this month's virtue. He liked to say that the tiny arms of the Infant, stretched wide in love, were the same arms that would one day be stretched out in love upon the Cross. Not hesitating to link up Christmas and Good Friday, he says: "The love which Jesus entertained for the cross was so great that he embraced it from the first moment of his incarnation. The will of his heavenly Father had decreed that his life on earth should be the way of the cross. Accordingly, he began his sorrowful journey to Calvary the very moment that he took flesh and dwelled among us. If we desire to be made conformable to the image of the Word Incarnate we too must love God's will and carry our cross with patience and resignation. For, 'he who will not take up his cross and come after me is not worthy of me' (Matthew 10:38)."

Why So Much Emphasis on the Cross?

I have a confession to make. From time to time, as I reflect on the writings of Saint Alphonsus, I find myself growing restive with his heavy emphasis on the cross. Why does he seem to emphasize suffering so much? What is so great about the cross? How can an average person be expected to love the cross?

In searching for an answer to these questions, it is necessary to take a longer look at several other questions, namely: What does Saint Alphonsus mean by "the cross"? What does he mean by "love of the cross"? How does love of the cross affect our lives?

What Is the Cross?

The cross, according to Saint Alphonsus, is a symbolic term that refers, quite simply, to the sufferings of human life. These may be either external or internal; they may be physical, psychological, spiritual. There is nothing mystical about them; they are very down-to-earth: for example, the loss of health, financial worries, emotional upheavals, the breakdown of relationships with family or friends, mental anguish, temptations to evil, spiritual dryness.

The basic conviction of Saint Alphonsus was that such suffering is an intimate part of every person's life, a reality that has to be dealt with in one way or another. Human experience, he wrote, teaches us that every life is touched by suffering. "All men must suffer, the just as well as the sinner. One is lacking in this, another is deprived of that. This person is intelligent but not wealthy; that person is rich but has no claim to knowledge; another is both intelligent and rich, but has lost his health. In a word all of us — rich or poor, learned or unlearned, sinners or saints — have something to suffer."

The key issue, then, is not whether we will suffer but how? There are, to be sure, many answers to this question. Some people become chronic complainers: they suffer all right, but they make sure everybody knows about it, all the time! Others make a career out of trying to avoid suffering: they are escape artists who free their hands from one cross — only to find them attached to another. (Saint Alphonsus wisely points out that "when we try to avoid a cross the Lord has sent us, we usually meet with another, and a much heavier one.") Still others grow bitter in suffering, alienated from God and from others, hardhearted and unloving.

What Is Love of the Cross?

The true Christian, according to Saint Alphonsus, should respond to the "how" of suffering by developing a love of the cross. When Saint Alphonsus speaks of love of the cross, however, he is not talking about some sadistic cult of pain. He is talking, rather, about a spirit of patience and conformity to God's will. He is talking about the spirit of Jesus in his suffering and death. "How is it possible to look at a crucifix and see the Christ who died in an ocean of sufferings without bearing patiently for love of him all the sufferings that God may choose to send us?"

This same spirit is graphically portrayed in the lives of the saints. Saint Alphonsus describes it this way: "If you read the lives of the saints, you will be astonished at the sufferings so many of them had to endure. These sufferings were like so many stepping-stones to love and to intimate union with God." For this reason Saint Alphonsus announced a principle that applies to every disciple of Christ: "The surest proof of genuine love of God is shown when we willingly embrace the cross that he sends us."

Translated into everyday life, this spirit will prompt us to bear our sufferings without complaint, without bitterness, without hardness of heart, without alienation from God. The spirit of Christ will teach us to bear the cross with gentleness, with cheerfulness, with equanimity, with love. Love of the cross is a positive response to the mandate of Jesus: "If a man wishes to come after me, he must deny his very self, take up his cross, and follow in my steps" (Mark 8:34).

How Does Love of the Cross Affect Our Lives?

Love of the cross affects our lives especially in two ways. First of all, those who grow in this virtue will soon begin to experience peace of heart. This peace, for which we are constantly searching, comes to us "only when we carry our cross with patience and resignation." Saint John of the Cross — the great master of contemplative prayer — points out that when we finally accept suffering in a gentle and patient spirit, then we will be able to say: "My house is now at rest."

Second, love of the cross enables us to share, in a mysterious way, in the redemptive mission of Jesus. Our sufferings take on new meaning. In the words of Saint Paul: "In my own flesh I fill up what is lacking in the sufferings of Christ for the sake of his body, the church" (Colossians 1:24).

Practical Suggestions

As we try to concentrate on love of the cross this month, we might find the following suggestions helpful:

First Week: Read in a prayerful manner the infancy narrative as described in chapters 1 and 2 of Saint Luke's Gospel, and the passion narrative as described in chapters 22 and 23 of the same Gospel.

Second Week: Pinpoint the most significant sufferings of our lives here and now: for example, poor health, emotional anguish, broken relationships, spiritual dryness.

Third Week: Ask ourselves: What is our most characteristic negative approach to our sufferings? Anger? Complaint? Bitterness? Ask ourselves: What is our most characteristic positive approach to our sufferings? Patience? Resignation? Love?

Fourth Week: Determine how we can become more positive and less negative in our sufferings. Pray daily for that grace.

Selected Bibliography

1. In our treatment of the virtue of Faith (January), one of the practical suggestions was to "set aside some time for enlarging or enriching our knowledge of God's revelation . . . This might include a planned reading of the Scriptures, a study of the Creed, or a fuller understanding of Catholic teaching as found, for example, in the documents of Vatican II or in a catechism for adults."

I would like now to suggest several resources that would be helpful in this effort:

- *Discovering the Bible,* Book One and Book Two, by Reverend John Tickle. Each of these books treats eight basic themes of the Bible, comparing them as they appear first in the Old Testament and then in the New Testament. These books are helpful for the Bible beginner and for the longtime Bible student. (Liguori Publications, $3.95 each)
- *Your Faith: A Practical Presentation of Catholic Belief and Sacramental Life.* This book provides an easy-to-understand yet comprehensive study of Catholicism. (Liguori Publications, $2.95)

2. As a follow-up to our treatment of Love of Neighbor (April) the following book provides many insights:

- *How to Deal with Difficult People,* by Andrew Costello, C.SS.R. (Liguori Publications, $2.95)

3. The virtue of Poverty (May) invites us to examine our consciences on issues of social justice and to apply the Gospel more fully in our lives. I recommend the following booklets as helpful aids:
- *The Bible, the Church, and Social Justice,* by Richard Schiblin, C.SS.R. Issues of injustice, poverty, and oppression are treated from the Christian viewpoint, and practical suggestions are offered. (Liguori Publications, $1.50)
- *Dare to Be Christian: Developing a Social Conscience,* by Bernard Häring, C.SS.R. A series of beautiful and challenging meditations for the Christian in today's world. (Liguori Publications, $4.25)

4. The treatment of the virtue of Chastity (June) touches lightly on several points that may be more fully explored in these writings:
- *Sexual Morality: Guidelines for Today's Catholic,* by Russell Abata, C.SS.R. (Liguori Publications, $1.50)
- *The Six Levels of a Happy Marriage,* by Reverend Medard Laz. (Liguori Publications, $1.50)

5. The favorite themes of Saint Alphonsus — the love of God, conformity to God's will, recollection and prayer, preparation for death — are contained in these selections of his writings:
- *Love Is Prayer/Prayer Is Love,* edited by John Steingraeber, C.SS.R. (Liguori Publications, $2.95)
- *How to Face Death Without Fear,* adapted by Norman Muckerman, C.SS.R. (Liguori Publications, $1.50)